T0029471

LEARNING TO SETTLE DOWN

LEARNING TO SETTLE DOWN

CHAD NORMAN

Black Moss
Press

2015

Library and Archives Canada Cataloguing in Publication

Norman, Chad, author
    Learning to settle down / Chad Norman.

Poems.
ISBN 978-0-88753-552-9 (paperback)

    I. Title.

PS8577.O469L43 2015   C811'.54   C2015-903879-0

Cover photo by Marty Gervais
Layout & design by Jay Rankin
Edited by Meghan Desjardins

Published by Black Moss Press at 2450 Byng Road, Windsor,
Ontario, N8W 3E8. Canada. Black Moss books are distributed in
Canada and the U.S. by Fitzhenry & Whiteside. All orders should
be directed there.
        Fitzhenry & Whiteside
        195 Allstate Parkway
        Markham, ON
        L3R 4T8

Black Moss
EST. 1969 **Press**

Black Moss would like to acknowledge the generous financial sup-
port from both the Canada Council for the Arts and the Ontario
Arts Council.

ONTARIO ARTS COUNCIL
CONSEIL DES ARTS DE L'ONTARIO
an Ontario government agency
un organisme du gouvernement de l'Ontario

Canada Council   Conseil des arts
for the Arts   du Canada

for Norm

*a man who has known how quick wonder
can appear and vanish.*

Contents

ANOTHER SEASON TRIES TO GROW THE GARDEN

CONVINCED OF THE VITALITY OF AN OPINION

FLOWERS

AND

FOOD

LOVE

A

HUMAN

How To Make A Tree Happy

Begin the cloudy morning
with a welcome
for the return of the leaves,
a welcome to include
a few moments of
whispering through a window,
no more effort than
to say, "I am glad you found
the way back to the branches,
the spots where you sprouted,
where on hotter days
you will become the reason
to forget money and failures,
and exit the house
to nap in the blessing of shade."

THE HOLLOW MEN FINALLY ARE FULFILLED

All is well
when the bees & butterflies
commingle on a breeze
in the garden.

BLESSING

Peace can
be found
in the sunlight
now catching
the snow
on a spruce's
bough.

Casa Harris
Truro, Nova Scotia
Dec. 8/09

A Brief Sigh

As the Earth ages
it becomes
less and less
about Birth.

Casa Harris
Dec. 10/09

13

THE SHAPE OF A PUDDLE

After so many years
a man
can walk by
a body of water
and have to admit
it will never be
more than a puddle.

However when
a certain morning
on the established way
to the job
causes him to notice
the puddle
has changed its shape
from a heart
to something resembling
his own genitalia
alarm is not with him.

It is simple
the sky wishes
a smaller
and more
controversial reflection.

Casa Harris
July 27/10

PERHAPS
for Sherry, on her birthday

To believe in what one sees
out of the corner of an eye,
a muted Calico cat on stairs,
someone or something
going by a window, or those
maple seeds hung out
in the backyard, possibly
seen, as the wind takes
them out of branches
and turns them into
twirling forms of some sort,
perhaps undiscovered insects
unallowed to land
in the unmown grass,
and, perhaps, take hold
to become what may be
a tree, or another mystery
there and gone in
a matter of believable moments.

Casa Harris
June 15/10

FROST ON A FINGERNAIL

One of the newer neighbours
after a special morning act,
simply getting out of bed
to escort a stepson,
a jaunt up the hill
ending where the sidewalk
changes from the public
to school-owned property,
turns from the hug
and the departure,
ready to return
for what could be
or absolutely should be
called a scene, between
a man and nature,
a scene
between a finger
and its cloudy nail
at the tip, where
after a short scrape
frost has coated
in all its fragile artwork
that annoying gift, yes,
the human fingernail,
called upon when the need
to scratch drives the neighbour

to heal himself briefly,
or before that pile of
stunning ice melts forever
and he asks to be with
a moment others missed,
due to typical choices
like reliance on a bus,
like rolling over to believe
the child will get there,
will make the bell on time.

Casa Harris
April 16/10

The Persistence Of A Miracle
for Paul Zann

Drops
must begin
it,
a beginning
only
when warmth
begins to end,
when drops
fall
into the
beginning
of a freeze,
drops
stopping to
become
an end
& a beginning
when warmth
ends,
in order
to form,
to be
a form
prepared to
become
a form

frozen,
drops freezing
when cold
secures
and holds
the first drops,
drops
which will
leave the form,
the clear form,
in order
to become
the beginning
of the end
of what
the drops
never knew they
were meant
to end up,
drops
once again
falling,
letting go
of a form,
drops
no longer
in need of
being
an icicle.

AFTER A BRIEF THOUGHT ABOUT BEING BLIND

for my mother, and all she has given

In the chilly kitchen
filling with the aroma
of toasted brown bread
the first break of sunlight
turns on an icicle
formed by the roof drain's leak.

So through the plastic blinds
a moment becomes all
when the watching begins,
to be a glad witness
with willing thankful eyes
as the first drop forms.

Casa Harris
Feb. 13/10

NOTHING BUT THE MOMENT
for Lainee

An aging man
has sat
and admired
the mist
longing to
be total rain.

Casa Harris
Nov. 25/09

THE IMPORTANCE OF LONGING
for Lin Yutang

No one
in particular
sips a
chilled Bavaria 8.6 Red
and longs
for the day
he no longer
misses
the leaves,
trying to
imagine what
it must be like
for the trees.

Casa Harris
April 1/10

Now We Play Outside

Sunlight in
raindrops on wires
allows a man
to stop a routine,

wind through
raindrops on wires
allows a boy
within the man

to imagine them,
the lights of traffic
on an undulating
bridge in a storm.

LEARNING TO SETTLE DOWN

After a day of
pushing the mower
over the lawn,
wiping a brow
more than once,
as the heat
somehow led him
to a hammer,
a fancy drill,
led him to build
a gate for the garden,
he washes his face
knowing
the yard is listening
to his yawn.

Casa Harris
July 4/10

WHAT COMPARES

How
the new leaves
feel
as soft as
a newborn's
earlobe.

on the way to the job
May 2010

A Symphony Of Creaks .

Rising, shift over,
walking out of,
stepping up the stairs
which bring him
up from the job
into a temperature
gone down in a day,
down to degrees
brought to the water
which will cause ice, a freeze
the wind is responsible for,
as he steps toward
the walk into trees,
a wind only branches know
as he steps upon white inches,
into streets where most waken,
into streets the houses protect,
away from the music of flakes,
a late season, away from
what he wants, some kind
of symphony, yes, a Beethoven
of creaks, the trees playing
like keys, a symphony of creaks.

written while walking home
Feb. 5/10

Park Bench As Pew

A frequent doubter
considers
the new snowfall
a new religion.

Casa Harris
Jan. 21/10

GAZE

A waking man
stops his life,
as somehow a lone
snowflake clings to
a strand of a web
long abandoned
by a neighbourhood spider
which also once knew
a few survival tips
about holding on to the wind.

Casa Harris
Jan. 21/10

THOUGHT UPON WAKING

Someone woke up
thinking about
the understanding
and trust
a raindrop
must have
while clinging to
a spruce needle.

Casa Harris
Nov. 21/09

Reliance

When the wind designates
a certain breeze
to carry an oak leaf
far enough over
the cedar boughs,
and finally settle it
in the scheduled snow's
first brief whitening.

Casa Harris
Nov. 9/09

Last Bastion Of The Absurd #1

Pausing,
one man thinks
another man's laughter
is a
seagull.

Casa Harris
Jan. 21/10

LAST BASTION OF THE ABSURD #2

The sound of
crows' wings
flapping past
is like an
old unshaven man
scratching
his cheeks and chin.

on the way to the job
May 2010

LAST BASTION OF THE ABSURD #3

The heart beating
in an ear
pushed against a pillow,
reminder
of the sound made
as two bodies
meet during
an afternoon
snuck in
for pleasure.

LAST BASTION OF THE ABSURD #4

In the neighbourhood
one morning
the employee
who takes the garbage
and shakes out
the town's compost bins
sounds like
the stereo's bass
in a new red
convertible Mustang
stopped at the
inaudible crosswalk.

Casa Harris
May 18/10

How To Save A Worm

Firstly
& most importantly
when you
come upon one
you
must stop your life.

Secondly
& equally importantly
when you
have your life stopped
you
must bend over
with fingers bared
& safely pick up
the tiny gelatinous being.

And thirdly
with a harmless hold
transport the wriggling,
the longing for soil,
off the drizzled street
back to
the green sanctity
of someone's
yielding front yard.

ALLOWED TO MARVEL

There is a person
alone
who is whispering
in a basement
for some reason,
perhaps if you
listen closer
this is all that's being said:
"What I would give
to sing for the sun
like the robins
at the moment,
this frosty sun-found
beginning of
another new morning
when I have been
allowed to marvel."

Casa Harris
April 14/10

36

Beyond The Yard

Someone
caught off guard,
as they say,
rejoices
as the crickets,
or perhaps, the frogs,
now rejoice,
safe in
the darkness
of another
early springtime
evening.

Casa Harris
April 10/10

BRIEF
for Jean Fisher

I admit
if I had to say
I know anything
about being alive,
it is that I know
the beautiful sounds
of a mother crow
of a mother crow
speaking to her grown baby,
out on some
nearby tree limb.

Casa Harris
July 15/11

ON

OCCASION

A

NAME

IS

DROPPED

Sunday Has No Ending

A wish,
to share some beauty:
there is bliss
while reading excerpts of Whitman,
as the book is painted
with the sun, and its shadows
swaying, due to the wind
in a browning lilac bush.

Casa Harris
Sept. 6/09

STRING ON A FINGER

Someone
sits in a sedated state,
completely overtaken
by the music of Miles Davis
and Jimi Hendrix.

As a reminder
when he or she is silenced,
please send either off
with CDs by both.
Please. Don't forget!

A Life Of Little

Some quiet man
once dared
to say very loudly,
I love two songs equally:
one, I think, I hope,
is called "Time Waits
For No One," and the other
I seem
to have forgotten.

On Finding A Treasure

How irresistible it became
not to the tell the world
as the sunflower
gave up each petal
upon landing they broke
into tiny yellow specks
covering the cracked case
of Bob Marley's *One Love* CD.

Casa Harris
Oct. 5/09

43

One Afternoon, Alone, & Amused

A semi-drunk fellow
rests in the front room
of his semi-cool home,
seeing a movie, *Sylvia*,
full of a feeling
he can describe as how
his garden must feel,
outside, temperature 30ºC,
adding to the ripening
of this year's wet & short
odd growing season.

The kind gardeners listen,
feel their garden's intent,
much like the growth of themselves.

SHAKING THE SHIFT

Someone may be free.
Someone may experience
a natural collaboration:
humming a Hendrix tune
walking away from the job,
walking under still leaves
both green and now red,
during the predicted rainfall.

Casa Harris
Sept. 24/09

It Is This Way

How to begin
a day:
all it takes
is
one song
by Antony,
and one
gentle reach
in
to take
the tear
from
a beard.

Casa Harris
July 19/10

BRAVO TO BRAVO TV
for P. Quarrington

Paul
is dead,
now.

He told
us about
whales,
their music.

That novel,
Des,
Claire,
how sad
the whales
were,
and perhaps,
still are.

Poems And The Whiteness Of Their Pages

The attempts,
he says,
attempts to deal with
Violation:

the defacement,
some academic's scribbled analysis
sadly throughout
an innocent copy of
T.S. Eliot's *Collected Poems*.

Casa Harris
Jan. 7/10

To Be A Man

After hearing
the words
and watching
the smiles
during a
Rosanne Cash
interview
he notices
the tears
asking something
of how he
has come to accept,
or even admire,
his present
manhood.

Casa Harris
May 14/10

A Meal Before Breakfast

A man alone
in a hungry part
of himself
begins the day with
the nutritious words
of Gwen MacEwen,
feeding the silence
already being fed
by the first sounds
of his family waking.

Casa Harris
Nov. 9/09

BENT HALO

One is certain
Hendrix while recording
his *Electric Ladyland* LP
spoke and played
for a future
he would've never
considered to be a Now.

THIS IS ONLY A TEST

I repeat,
this only a test,
we are
under attack
by our own
Prime Minister.
Please vacate
any thoughts of
a better or sensible
government.
I repeat…

To Tell No Tale

A man
confesses,
as of late there is
but one bird
to set
upon his shoulder,
and that is
Bird Parker.

Casa Harris
Oct. 4/09

Remembering Irina Ratushinskaya

Dare to imagine
during the age of Gorbachev
a poet was
writing poems,
while being charged
and incarcerated (in a camp)
for writing poems
on bars of soap, somehow
each one carved
with a burnt matchstick.

ANOTHER
SEASON
TRIES
TO
GROW
THE
GARDEN

Snow On Sunflowers #1

A rain, a gale, a change,
why succumb to the pain
the mind wants to suggest
the body situates, falls
down to, the pain left
simply by being alive,
throwing oneself into
being the lifeful one?

Now that it is washed off,
all those significant flakes,
it is rinsed away, rain and
all those shapes in a drain,
nothing about the flower
remains, other than months
of a man and his choices
to allow a yellow rope
to hold up what once was
yellow petals, and promises
of food for birds
through a winter which
has overtaken, hasn't spread
the freeze in so deep
that a garden
can be forgotten.

Casa Harris
Jan. 28/10

Snow On Sunflowers #2
for Cory S.

Across from the petals,
the sun-lured petals,
yellow in their own way,
more than one snowflake
has attached itself, if a
snowflake may be a self,
to all the expanse, the
surface of seeds, unripened,
white-like, well, no different
from the snow, a fall from
clouds once pushed aside
by a heat the sun
kept private for another
season, in honour, quietly,
but unquestionably, of the
Winter.

Casa Harris
Jan. 28/10

Snow On Sunflowers #3

There is a ponderous man
who
after a healing shower
sits
in the chill of a basement
gathering
thoughts of peace
from a recent storm,
the white
accumulation
outside on bent stalks,
resting and melting
between
black and white seeds
pecked
before being picked.

Blue Jays In The Sunflowers

A quiet man
decided to remain quiet
after one of you
hit his front window.

What he discovered then
would be between him
and the lies of that glass.
His awe had really never died.

A discovery he saw as similar
to what you were left with
lying stunned in the boughs,
the trusty cedar grown
to shelter you.

At times, a moment
or longer, the feeling
of helplessness, real,
and deep inside him,
a man who decided
to believe in
and stay out of what
Nature eventually brought.
A healing, a destination
reached, sunflowers

ripened for the day's hunger
where your mate was waiting.

Casa Harris
Dec. 23/09

To Let The Garden Go
for Dennis B.

Such immediate sadness,
an unexpected growth
late in the season.

Crops gone, left with
what frost turns plants into,

those your hands started
by cautiously placing seeds
into an earth,

so wonderfully willing
to begin the gardener,

now only a feeling,
only a longing to return
to what never was,

a gardener, a hope, a seed,

just a possibility,
just a man,
alone, with thoughts of eating.

Casa Harris
Oct. 15/09

How It Blows

A pondering gardener
nears the end of a day
full of many forms of teachings,
all of which come from
the wind, and sunflowers
the wind has caused to leave
their brittle umbilical stalks.

Casa Harris
Sept. 30/09

A Day Off Of Time

A rare morning:
stillness.

To allow a mosquito
to drink,

while picking
ripened tomatoes & beans,

accompanied by a fog
deeper than usual,

and pleasingly uninterested
in any lifting.

Casa Harris
Sept. 21/09

EARLY DARKNESS

Once more, a boy
has felt the determination
of a sizable grasshopper
in his cupped hands
to locate a way back
to the yellow gladiola,
now, petal by petal,
taking on a bit of mist.

WHEN NIGHT GIVES WAY TO MORNING

An admission:
he hadn't kissed
anyone or anything
until he kissed
the face of a sunflower
after an evening of frost.

Casa Harris
Sept. 11/09

SUMMER GOING SOMEWHERE

Tips of
the new yellow beans
now touch
tips of the lawn's
dry unmown
blades of grass.

A Gentle Removal

The first of blooms,
white rolling up out the middle,
mauve alongside the white,
darker purple on petal edges,
taken from gladiola stem,
picked, hopefully, to lounge long
in the red wooden bowl
hardly full of country water.

A VANTAGE POINT

Simply wandering
throughout
the rain-dotted leaves
of the July garden,
long after the job's backshift
was kindly over,
the lone grasshopper,
translucently green,
looking like the newest
to join the growing,
sat in the middle
of a stake for
the tomatoes, a
stake which last year
was the stalk of
a twelve-foot
sunflower plant,
sat in the middle
on what would be
the cambium, the marrow,
where the water
once climbed to
quench a flower's thirst,
and all the seeds
it eventually gave to
the relentless, hestitant,
blue jays.

CONVINCED
OF
THE
VITALITY
OF
AN
OPINION

No Response

Silence
was never meant
to be an excuse
for anyone
who cannot say, "No."

Those counting on it,
silence, violate what
some of us use
as religion, Silence.

Please speak when
an answer must be spoken.

LEFT WITH A GRIN

All the time
waiting for the mail
it had already been delivered—
envelopes now
anticipating his arrival.

THE BRIEF INBETWEEN

A daring father
stands at that midpoint
where the festivities
must become the past
and the blurry challenges
of a new year arrive.
He (yes, sad, yet curious)
turns to adjust his vision,
to step into a new Unknown.

Casa Harris
Jan. 3/09

A Wish For Always

A man of well-being
had a wish,
a wish for always,
that someone
when he has left his life
will say,
"I knew him,
and knew him well."

During his living,
his fierce surviving,
that is all he wished:
to be,
and to be known
by someone.

Casa Harris
March 28/10

BERRY FILLED

Somehow
after the syrup
settled,
a smile
formed on
the purple pancake.

SILLY BILLY

All day
he sits long,
he sits quietly,
in front of
his many
dependable
Screens.

HOMAGE TO ARSEN PAYNE

A boy with
a billion toys
is bored.

In Need Of A Light

The boy in
a man's healthy body
seems to require
better eyesight
while attempting to
discover just when a
spider's web breaks
after the heater
is turned on.

Casa Harris
Nov. 25/09

Xia

for Terry & Theresa

Little daughter
asleep in the car seat
mother set you in,
a place of safety and a nap.

Little passenger
alive outside the womb
father got you to,
a room of growth and an exit.

Little sister
adored for the smiles
all see you give,
a view of peace and a life.

Little messenger
able to reassure a man
evening brought you once,
a soul of toil and a thank you.

Casa Harris
Sept. 2009

ONE OF MAYBE JUST ANOTHER

1. A theft took place
in the shadow of
a long barren tree.

To comment on more
could suggest he knew
little about detail & silence.

Time & days off led
to the discovery, the withheld,
the shadow said to be
a thief, & all is done.

2. A theft took place:
she saw a hand
thrust, foolishly, in a pocket,
clasping the lifted beer.

She saw it, she saw
a theft taking place
as he paid his way
through a door
she allowed to remain
an exit, unlocked,
quite contrary to her training.

Casa Harris
Jan. 7/10

THE PROVIDERS

A cold & tired body
has each of them behind a window;
however, they love how
the heat at the base of
dormant backyard trees
can & does melt the snow,
and then mislead their minds
with thoughts of Spring,
due to their dubious eyes,
focussed on what little of
the land is now revealed,
even though the colour green
must be considered
a momentary reminiscence.

Casa Harris
Feb. 23/10

The Marriage

A wife
is seated
in the living room:
there is no chair,
there is no furniture.

She is fully clothed
seated on the floor,
her legs
straight out
in front of her.

She sits in a square
of light
coming in the window;
the day is almost over,
the square
is shrinking,
the square
is an odd spotlight.

A wife
is seated
in a darkening room:
her face
the last of her body
left in the orange light.

There is a smile,
there is a finger
beckoning,
now that a new night
frees her.

Casa Harris
March 4/10

THE NAIL BITER

Three fingers are chosen,
two thumbs,
one a baby.

After the euphoric chew,
the bounty
is placed on a leg
clothed in black denim.

Two discardable nails,
like ragged straight lines.

And the remarkable third,
shaped like a smile
which can be stashed
in a shirt pocket,

for a day in the future
when a sadness
clips another shape
onto the lips.

Casa Harris
March 7/10

83

THE LOST WINDOW

Imagine one with no home,
no handy garage,
no seaside cottage,
no trusty outhouse.

Imagine one on the ground,
leaning against a wall,
far from any office building,
or fancy restaurant,
or nearby pizza joint.

Imagine one without
a pair of eyes,
human eyes,
one without
a single soul.

Casa Harris
March 10/10

ALIVE

At the point
when a man
opens both eyes
in order to adjust
to another greeting,
his presence
and a ceiling,
he marvels
at the body
which houses
the occupant
he is.

Casa Harris
March 12/10

A Tiny Bit Of Gall, Perhaps

Just for this morning
a bold thought
to redefine joy
as really nothing
to do with being human,
simply, instead,
the sun in the steam
it has caused
to waltz across
the frosty shingles
of a neighbour's roof.

Casa Harris
March 17/10

The Home Owner

"There,
that is my yard,
there,
that is my property.
Money says
I must believe this,
I must believe
I own that land."

What the man alone
says,
what the man at peace
says,
to himself
after the window
has been opened,
has been stood in front of,
opened to
welcome a new season,
a season
with a promise
of much needed heat,
heat sent
to alter the overclothed body,
to alter
the chilled being

ready to elbow the sun
to cause at least one chuckle.

Casa Harris
Mar. 19/10

A Rare Type Of Sympathy #1

Poor towel,
it is
never dry.

Casa Harris
Mar. 20/10

A RARE TYPE OF SYMPATHY #2

See how
the rejection slip
can be blown
away
with just
one breath.

Casa Harris
Mar. 20/10

THE MAKING OF A PATH

Surely
we don't
all
have to
be
guided by
lines
and
signs.

Casa Harris
April 1/10

DRUNK BEFORE A FLIGHT

The little girl
stares up at him,

his hands folded
as if about to pray.

She turns now
to stare
across the table
at her mother.

She folds
her hands
& the family
quickly says
grace.

Toronto Airport
4:25pm
April 10/06

No Doctor Necessary

After soaking
flat aching feet
in hot smelly water
he dries them
in a damp white towel
and relief
moves through him
to become
what may be calm,
or a few thoughts
on how a lot of his life
is where it should be,
and when he stands
there is a brief healing,
yes, to be upright,
the weight of the body
leaving a room,
worry somehow replaced
by a simple tingling
in the tip of each toe.

Casa Harris
May 13/10

WHITE HAND IN THE BLACK HAND

Speaking to himself
in the heat
of the Age,
he, accepting of
the choice
to attempt
to live seeing
skin as
no reference
to any colours,
speaks to himself,
one on
one planet,
alone with as much as
time allows,
food allows,
shelter allows,
alone, one in skin,
knowing to speak
will cause something,
will cause his hand
to remain an offering.

Casa Harris
May 20/10

Marriage At The Five Year Mark

As he
hung out the wash
it was his briefs
pinned
by her panties
that made him
say, "Wow, we
sure have gotten
ourselves in
and out of things."

Casa Harris
June 18/10

A Life's Work

After you have read
a lot of books
in the bathtub
you get to know
the feel of
two pages
stuck together.

Casa Harris
June 28/10

Keeping Perfection Attainable

A green t-shirt
sporting a
breast pocket
strong enough
to hold a
notebook, a
cheap pen,
and a few
recent poems
folded to fit.

Casa Harris
July 4/10

97

OK, PART ONE

There is no
real healing
until
one is
dead.

OK, Part Two

The eye
must see
when
the pupil
has
been tested.

ALL CLOCKS MUST FACE THE WALL

Some unsure person
hopes others more certain
gladly accept
belief in a joy
sent by an acceptance:
they may now be
on their own hour.

Casa Harris
Dec. 4/09

SUPERHEROES FART TOO

At nine
a boy
asks why
they, well,
some of them,
no longer
say, "Excuse me."

THERE'S NO CHOICE LIKE IT
for Jeremy

War is
a place of business
where he or she
chooses to sign up,
set to seek a trade,
all in all
where, if lucky,
service
is spent repairing
wornout possibilities.

Casa Harris
July 4/10

AFTER SPRING ENTERS THE ROOM

Strangely life,
our chase for money,
stops, to become
another life
when upon noticing
trees once barren
during the drag of winter,
blowing in breezes
brought to celebrate leaves,
trees not truly tree,
swaying, pleasing the eyes,
ask a certain man
to understand briefly
there is more to living
on the planet our feet knows
but is unable to explain,
due to the chase,
all that futility
the wind, the leaves, the branches
do not bow down to.

LISTENING TO OTHER THAN HUMANS

Each year
he comes upon
an empty
half shell,
once a
robin's egg.

What are
the crows
trying
to teach?

Casa Harris
July 12/10

Pondering The Meaning Of Christmas

Perhaps
the colour of
an occupied womb
resembles
the light of
a computer screen
left on
in a newly
decorated
living room.

An Unnecessary Rescue

Bath water, what
turns a man's skin
red, faster than
his embarrassment.

Once soaking, he is ready,
ready to read a book;
he has read thousands
in the tub, with skin
growing red, and the tub
full now, slowly steaming.

He reads the life of Thomas Hardy.

All the smooth whiteness
exhibits the lone drop,
the lone drinking ant.

Ant and a single drop,
water again causing life.

Ant able to hold on
where the tub's top slopes down:
holding on, one speck-like drop
on the edge of the slope
above the water able to change

what the human fingers
choose to rescue, to interfere with,
leaving the drop simply drank from,
to interfere and injure some part
of the ant's one innocent leg.

ACKNOWLEDGMENTS

Some of these poems have appeared in the following publications:
>Literary Review of Canada
>Pacific Rim Review of Books

First, I would like to thank Barton Cutten for helping to build the garden plots in my yard, which allowed me to once again put on the hat of the gardener. A chance to not only begin to feed my family vegetables I grew with my own hands, but also bringing the Muse of this book into my life, known to me as Awe.

I wish to thank Ruth, an unmistakably kind woman, who allowed me to take short-cuts through a small urban wooded lot she owns: a very generous place, where a number of these poems were found, or actually written, during walks to and from my paycheque, punch-the-clock job.

I also wish to thank Meghan Desjardins at Black Moss Press, for her incredible dedication to this book, and constant promptness, as well as welcomed skills as editor.

Another thank you goes out to Marty Gervais for his much appreciated choice to invite me into the Black Moss family.

And, finally, my wife, Lainee, for the "getting easier" task of putting up with me.

ABOUT THE AUTHOR

Chad Norman enjoys the pace living beside the
Atlantic.

Over the years he has published in many journals
in several countries, occasionally making it into one
which actually pays a few dollars.

He is a member of the League of Canadian Poets
and the Writers' Federation of Nova Scotia, always
happy to secure a reading or two somewhere in
Canada.

His most recent books are *Hugging The Huge Father*
(Expanded Version, 2012), a celebration of boys,
sons, fathers, and men, and *Masstown* (Black Moss
Press, 2013).

Happily he assures us his love of walks remains
endless.